William Walton

BELSHAZZAR'S FEAST

FOR MIXED CHOIR
BARITONE SOLO
AND ORCHESTRA

VOCAL SCORE
REVISED EDITION 1955

Music Department
OXFORD UNIVERSITY PRESS
Oxford and New York

Printed in Great Britain by
William Clowes Ltd.
Beccles, Suffolk

Belshazzar's Feast

———

Thus spake Isaiah:

Thy sons that thou shalt beget
They shall be taken away,
And be eunuchs
In the palace of the King of Babylon
Howl ye, howl ye, therefore:
For the day of the Lord is at hand!

By the waters of Babylon,
By the waters of Babylon
There we sat down: yea, we wept
And hanged our harps upon the willows.

For they that wasted us
Required of us mirth;
They that carried us away captive
Required of us a song.
Sing us one of the songs of Zion.

How shall we sing the Lord's song
In a strange land?

If I forget thee, O Jerusalem,
Let my right hand forget her cunning.
If I do not remember thee,
Let my tongue cleave to the roof of my mouth.
Yea, if I prefer not Jerusalem above my chief joy.

By the waters of Babylon
There we sat down: yea, we wept.

O daughter of Babylon, who art to be destroyed,
Happy shall he be that taketh thy children
And dasheth them against a stone,   .
For with violence shall that great city Babylon be thrown down
And shall be found no more at all.

Babylon was a great city,
Her merchandise was of gold and silver,
Of precious stones, of pearls, of fine linen,
Of purple, silk and scarlet,
All manner vessels of ivory,
All manner vessels of most precious wood,
Of brass, iron and marble,
Cinnamon, odours and ointments,
Of frankincense, wine and oil,
Fine flour, wheat and beasts,
Sheep, horses, chariots, slaves
And the souls of men.

.   .   .   .

In Babylon
    Belshazzar the King
    Made a great feast,
Made a feast to a thousand of his lords,
And drank wine before the thousand.

Belshazzar, whiles he tasted the wine,
Commanded us to bring the gold and silver vessels:
Yea! the golden vessels, which his father, Nebuchadnezzar,
Had taken out of the temple that was in Jerusalem.

He commanded us to bring the golden vessels
Of the temple of the house of God,
That the King, his Princes, his wives
And his concubines might drink therein.

Then the King commanded us:
Bring ye the cornet, flute, sackbut, psaltery
And all kinds of music: they drank wine again,
Yea, drank from the sacred vessels,
And then spake the King:

iv

Praise ye
    The God of Gold
Praise ye
    The God of Silver
Praise ye
    The God of Iron
Praise ye
    The God of Wood
Praise ye
    The God of Stone
Praise ye
    The God of Brass
Praise ye the Gods!

Thus in Babylon, the mighty city,
Belshazzar the King made a great feast,
Made a feast to a thousand of his lords
And drank wine before the thousand.

Belshazzar whiles he tasted the wine
Commanded us to bring the gold and silver vessels
That his Princes, his wives and his concubines
Might rejoice and drink therein.

After they had praised their strange gods,
The idols and the devils,
False gods who can neither see nor hear,
Called they for the timbrel and the pleasant harp
To extol the glory of the King.
Then they pledged the King before the people,
Crying, Thou, O King, art King of Kings:
O King, live for ever . . .

And in that same hour, as they feasted
Came forth fingers of a man's hand
And the King saw
The part of the hand that wrote.

And this was the writing that was written:
'MENE, MENE, TEKEL UPHARSIN'
'THOU ART WEIGHED IN THE BALANCE
    AND FOUND WANTING'.
In that night was Belshazzar the King slain
And his Kingdom divided.

Then sing aloud to God our strength:
Make a joyful noise unto the God of Jacob.
Take a psalm, bring hither the timbrel,
Blow up the trumpet in the new moon,
Blow up the trumpet in Zion
For Babylon the Great is fallen, fallen.
                              Alleluia!

Then sing aloud to God our strength:
Make a joyful noise unto the God of Jacob,
While the Kings of the Earth lament
And the merchants of the Earth
Weep, wail and rend their raiment.
They cry, Alas, Alas, that great city,
In one hour is her judgement come.

The trumpeters and pipers are silent,
And the harpers have ceased to harp,
And the light of a candle shall shine no more.

Then sing aloud to God our strength.
Make a joyful noise to the God of Jacob.
For Babylon the Great is fallen.
                              Alleluia!

Selected and arranged from
the Bible by
OSBERT SITWELL

The orchestral score and parts may be hired from the publishers. Copies of the vocal score also are available for hire. Terms on application.

The full score is published, (Imp. 8vo)

ORCHESTRA

Flute I
Flute II
Piccolo

Oboe I
Oboe II

(Cor Anglais: only in absence of Saxophone)

Clarinet I in B♭
Clarinet in E♭, doubling
Clarinet II in B♭
Bass Clarinet, doubling
Clarinet III in B♭

Alto Saxophone in E♭

Fagotto I
Fagotto II
Contra Fagotto

4 Horns in F (Cor.)

3 Trumpets
2 Tenor Trombones
1 Bass Trombone
Tuba

Timpani: 3, or preferably 4 (one player)

Percussion: 3, or preferably
   4 players:
Side Drum (Tamb. Mil.)
Tenor Drum
Triangle
Tambourine
Castanets
Cymbals
Bass Drum (G.C.)
Gong
Xylophone
Glockenspiel
Wood Block
Slapsticks
Anvil

2 Harps

Pianoforte (ad lib.)

Organ

Strings

Two Brass Bands, (optional) one to the left and one to the right of the Conductor each consisting of:

3 Trumpets
2 Tenor Trombones
1 Bass Trombone
1 Tuba
(The Trombones and Tuba parts are cued in the Orchestral Trombone and Tuba parts.)

To Lord Berners

Belshazzar's Feast

For Mixed Choir, Baritone Solo and Orchestra

Text arranged from Biblical sources by
OSBERT SITWELL

WILLIAM WALTON

Notes in small type in the voice parts refer to the German text only, by Beryl de Zoete and Baronin Imma Doernberg (revised **1951**)

king of Ba - by-lon. Howl_ ye, howl_ ye, there-fore; For the
Kö-nig zu Ba - by-lon! Heu - let, heu - let, da - rum; denn der

king of Ba - by-lon. Howl_ ye, howl_ ye, there-fore; For the
Kö-nig zu Ba - by-lon! Heu - let, heu - let, da - rum; denn der

day of the Lord_ is at hand._
Tag des Ge - rich-tes ist nah'!_

day of the Lord_ is at hand._
Tag des Ge - rich-tes ist nah'!_

6

TENORI

TENORI

BASSI

SOPRANI

CONRALTI

TENORI

div. *p*

For they, they that
Denn die, so uns

BASSI

p

For they, they that
Denn die, so uns

4 * *inquietamente*

4 * *inquietamente*

* There is a graduated 'più mosso' from **4** where ♩ = **63**(circa) to the eleventh bar after **5** where ♩ = **126** (circa)

* *Von* **4** *wo* ♩ = **63** *(circa) ein ansteigendes 'più mosso' beginnt bis zum elften Takt nach* **5** *bis* ♩ = **126** *(circa)*

8

II

12

13

14

*at this point the whole choir is to divide into two choruses.
Hier trennt sich der ganze Chor in zwei Chöre.

CHORUS I

Oh Je - ru - sa - lem, Oh Je -
O Je - ru - sa - lem, O Je -

Oh Je - ru - sa - lem, Oh Je -
O Je - ru - sa - lem, O Je -

Oh Je - ru - sa - lem, Oh Je -
O Je - ru - sa - lem, O Je -

Oh Je - ru - sa - lem, Oh Je -
O Je - ru - sa - lem, O Je -

CHORUS II

- ru - sa - lem, Oh Je - ru -
- ru - sa - lem, O Je - ru -

- ru - sa - lem, Oh Je -
- ru - sa - lem, O Je -

- ru - sa - lem, Oh Je - ru -
- ru - sa - lem, O Je - ru -

- ru - sa - lem, Oh Je - ru -
- ru - sa - lem, O Je - ru -

8

22

13 meno mosso poco a poco con rubato

more at all.
mehr, nie mehr. _____

_____ no more at all.
zu fin - den sein.

BARITONE SOLO
Quasi recit. ad lib.
robusto

Ba - by-lon __ was a great _____ ci - ty, her merchandise was of gold and sil-ver,
Ba - by-lon __ war eine gros - se Stadt. Sie han-del-te __ mit Gold und Silber,

of prec-ious stones, of pearls, of fine lin-en, of pur-ple, silk, and scar-let, all man-ner
köst-li-chem Gestein, Per-len, fei-nem Lin-nen, mit Pur-pur, Seid' und Scharlach, al - ler-lei

ves-sels of i - vo-ry, All man-ner ves-sels of most precious wood, of brass, i - ron and mar-ble,
Ge-fäss aus El-fenbein, al - ler-lei Ge-fäss aus ed-lem Holz, aus Erz, Ei-sen und Mar-mor,

cin-na-mon, o-dours and oint-ments of Frankincense, wine and oil, fine flour, wheat and beasts, sheep,
mit Zimmet, Bal-sam und Sal-ben, mit Spe-ze-rein, Wein und Öl, mit Mehl, Mais, Rin-dern, und

meno mosso

hors - es, cha - riots, slaves, and the souls _____ of men. __
Ros - sen, Wa - gen, Sklaven und den See - len der Menschen.

*Accidentals only apply to the notes they precede.
Die Versetzungszeichen beziehen sich nur auf die ihnen nachhergehenden Noten.

tast-ed the wine comd-man-ed us to
trunken er war be-fahl er uns zu

tast-ed the wine comd-man-ed us to
trunken er war be-fahl er uns zu

tast-ed the wine Com-mand ed us, com-mand-ed us to
trunken er war Be-fahl er uns, be-fahl er uns zu

tast-ed the wine Com-mand ed us, com-mand-ed us to
trunken er war Be-fahl er uns, be-fahl er uns zu

17

bring the gold and sil-ver ves-sels, Yea, the gold-en ves-sels which his fa-ther
brin-gen Gold-und Sil-ber - be-cher, gol - de-ne Ge-fäs-se die sein Va-ter

bring the gold and sil-ver ves-sels, Yea, the gold-en ves-sels which his fa-ther
brin-gen Gold-und Sil-ber - be-cher, gol - de-ne Ge-fäs-se die sein Va-ter

bring the gold and sil-ver ves-sels, Yea, the gold-en ves-sels which his fa-ther
brin-gen Gold-und Sil-ber - be-cher, gol - de-ne Ge-fäs-se die sein Va-ter

bring the gold and sil-ver ves-sels, Yea, the gold-en ves-sels which his fa-ther
brin-gen Gold-und Sil-ber - be-cher, gol - de-ne Ge-fäs-se die sein Va-ter

42

SOPRANI

Praise ___
Lo - bet,

CONTRALTI I

Praise ___
Lo - bet,

CONTRALTI II

30

ye   the god   of wood,
preist   des Hol - zes Gott!

ye   the god   of wood,
preist   des Hol - zes Gott!

56

58

60

63

BARITONE SOLO

And in that same hour as they feast - - ed came forth fin-gers of a man's hand
E-ben zu der sel - bi-gen Stun - - de er-schie-nen Finger ei-ner er Hand

And the King saw the part of the hand that wrote
und der König ward ge-wahr der Hand die schrieb

lunga **52**

♩ = 48

lugubre

ppp

Cym. G.C. Timp. Gong

8ve basso..........................

And this was the writing that was written—
und fol-gen-des war dort ge-schrieben:

'Me - ne,   me - ne,
Me - ne,   me - ne,

sim.

8ve..........................

53

te - kel u - phar - - sin.'
te - kel u - phar - - sin,

8ve..........................

*If performed in German, Chorus (T. I & II, B. I & II) sings this and the following bar

84

*Approximately one third of the full Choir.

92

98

CHORUS I

- ia,   Al-le -lu - ia,   Al-le-
- ia,   Al-le -lu - ia,   Al-le-

- ia,   Al - le - lu - ia,   Al - le -
- ia,   Al - le - lu - ia,   Al - le -

- ia,   Al - le - lu - ia,   Al - le -
- ia,   Al - le - lu - ia,   Al - le -

Al - le - lu - ia,   Al - le -
Al - le - lu - ia,   Al - le -

CHORUS II

Al-le - lu - ia,   Al-le-lu - ia,
Al-le - lu - ia,   Al le-lu - ia.

Al - le - lu - ia,   Al - le - lu - ia,
Al - le - lu - ia,   Al - le - lu - ia,

Al - le - lu - ia,   Al - le - lu - ia,
Al - le - lu - ia,   Al - le-- lu - ia,

- lu - ia,   Al - le - lu - ia,
- lu - ia,   Al - le - lu - ia,

106

III

77

Al - le - lu - ia, Al - le - lu - ia, Al - le -
Al - le - lu - ia, *Al - le - lu - ia,* *Al - le -*

Al - le - lu - ia, Al - le - lu - ia,
Al - le - lu - ia, *Al - le - lu - ia,*

- lu - ia,
- lu - ia,

ffp

Al - le - lu - - - - -
Al - le - lu - - - - -

ffp